AF338136

PUT IT IN THE ZOO!

Animal Book of Records
Children's Animal Books

Speedy Publishing LLC

40 E. Main St. #1156

Newark, DE 19711

www.speedypublishing.com

Copyright 2017

People collect animals in zoos so people can marvel at them and learn about them, and sometimes to protect rare animals from becoming extinct. Here are some record animals, and where you might want to go to see more.

THE OLDEST

Zoos try to provide ideal conditions for their animals, giving them the food they need and also the sort of medical care and attention they would never get in the wild. Animals lose their freedom, but they often gain a longer life to enjoy. Here are some of the oldest zoo animals.

Flamingo

GREATER THE FLAMINGO

Greater lived at the Adelaide Zoo in Australia until the age of 83. By that time the bird was nearly blind, and was suffering from arthritis that meant it could barely walk.

HARRIET
THE TORTOISE

Harriet was not the oldest tortoise ever known, as one in India may have reached the remarkable age of 250. However, Harriet, a Galapagos tortoise, did not do too badly: she was about 176 years old when she died in 2006 at a zoo in Queensland, Australia.

Tortoise

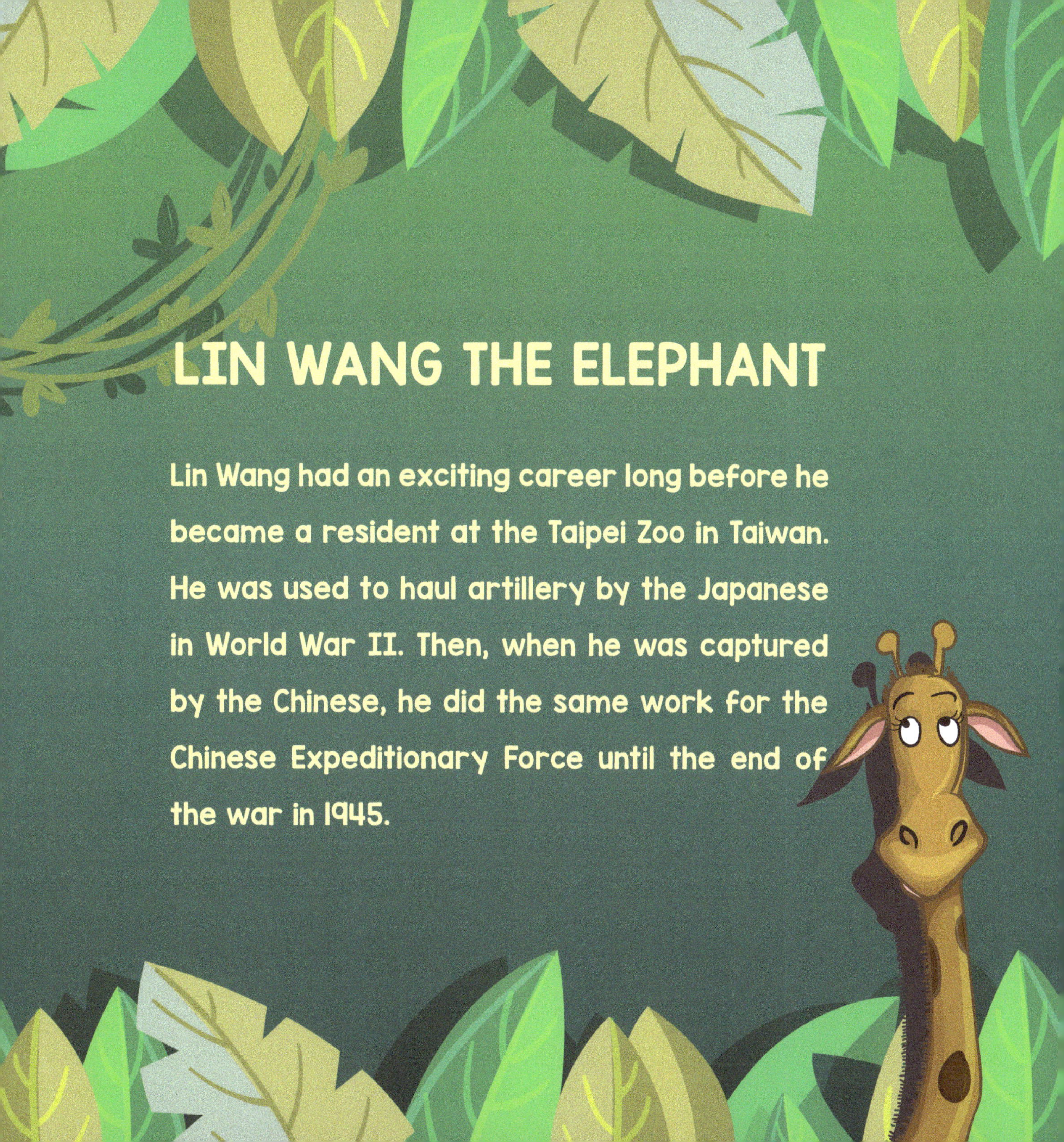

LIN WANG THE ELEPHANT

Lin Wang had an exciting career long before he became a resident at the Taipei Zoo in Taiwan. He was used to haul artillery by the Japanese in World War II. Then, when he was captured by the Chinese, he did the same work for the Chinese Expeditionary Force until the end of the war in 1945.

In 1952, at age 35, Lin Wang moved to the Taipei Zoo. There he met another elephant, Malan, who became his partner for the rest of their lives. Elephants usually live about fifty years, but Lin Wang just went on living. He became one of the favorite attractions at the zoo, with thousands of visitors who called him "Granpa".

Lin Wang died at age 86, in 2003. Tens
of thousands of people attended his
memorial service.

A VENERABLE TUATARA

Tuataras are lizards native to New Zealand and other islands of the South Pacific. They are now extremely rare. The oldest tuatara lived more than 117 years, and spent much of his life at the Southland Museum in New Zealand. He became a father for the first time when he was already over 110 years old!

Tuatara

The next six animals were not only the oldest zoo animals of their kind as of 2015: they were all neighbors at the Oregon Zoo in the United States.

INJI,
THE SUMATRAN ORANGUTAN

Inji may be the oldest Sumatran orangutan on Earth, not just in a zoo, at age 57. She takes aspirin for joint pain, but has no other serious medical problems. Inji was born around 1960, in the wild, and was donated to the zoo in 1961. Inji was captured for the pet trade business, which was legal at the time. Ending hunting animals to be sold as pets is a major piece of keeping species from becoming extinct.

Sumatran Orangutan

PACKY,
THE ASIAN ELEPHANT

Packy is 55, and is perhaps the tallest Asian elephant in the United States. He weighs over six tons. Packy was born in captivity, and is the oldest male Asian elephant in captivity.

HERMOSA,
THE HUMBOLDT PENGUIN

Hermosa was 33 in 2015 and beginning to suffer from age-related illnesses. Humboldt penguins only live about 20 years in their natural territory on the west coast of South America. She is too old to lay eggs now, but she acts as foster-mother for eggs laid by other penguins. Learn more about warm-water penguins in the Baby Professor book Penguins Like Warm Climates, Too!

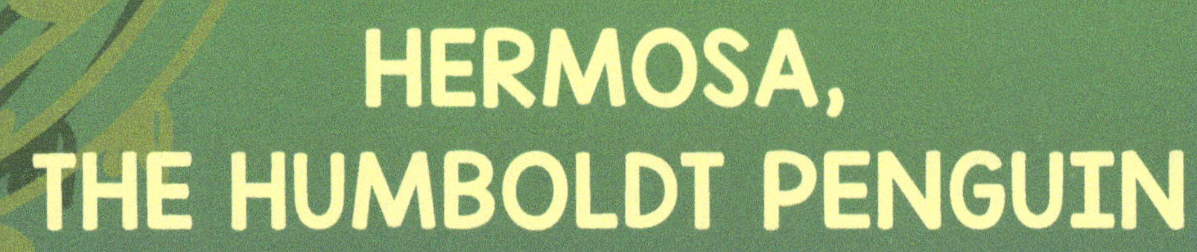

Humboldt Penguin

CONRAD,
THE POLAR BEAR

Conrad weighs over a thousand pounds and, at more than 30 years old, enjoys life at the zoo. Polar bears rarely live beyond 20 years, so Conrad is remarkable both for his age and for his youthful, playful nature.

KIA,
THE AMUR LEOPARD

Amur leopards are the world's most endangered big cats, and there are fewer than 100 left in their traditional area in southeast Russia. Kia is over 20, much older than the standard age for the leopards, and has given birth to ten babies. Read about the big cats in the Baby Professor book My Pet Cat Has Wild Cousins.

Amur Leopard

Lesser Flamingo

BIG PINK,
THE LESSER FLAMINGO

Big Pink was born around 1966, and at over 50 years old, is the oldest lesser flamingo in North America. He first lived at the San Antonio Zoo, and then moved to the Oregon Zoo in 2013. Lesser flamingos are the smallest flamingo species, and also are the brightest pink in color!

Zoos are often homes to rare animals, sometimes animals whose wild population is under threat. Zoos and wildlife sanctuaries preserve species whose habitat has been destroyed, or who have been hunted almost out of existence.

Albino Alligator

ALBINO AMERICAN ALLIGATOR

Newport Aquarium in Kentucky has a pair of rare white alligators. There are fewer than 200 albino alligators in the whole world.

AFRICAN PAINTED DOG

The Cincinnati Zoo in Ohio has several African painted dogs, a beautiful species that is known as a fierce hunter. There are fewer than three thousand of these dogs in the wild in Africa.

African Painted Dog

Snow Leopard

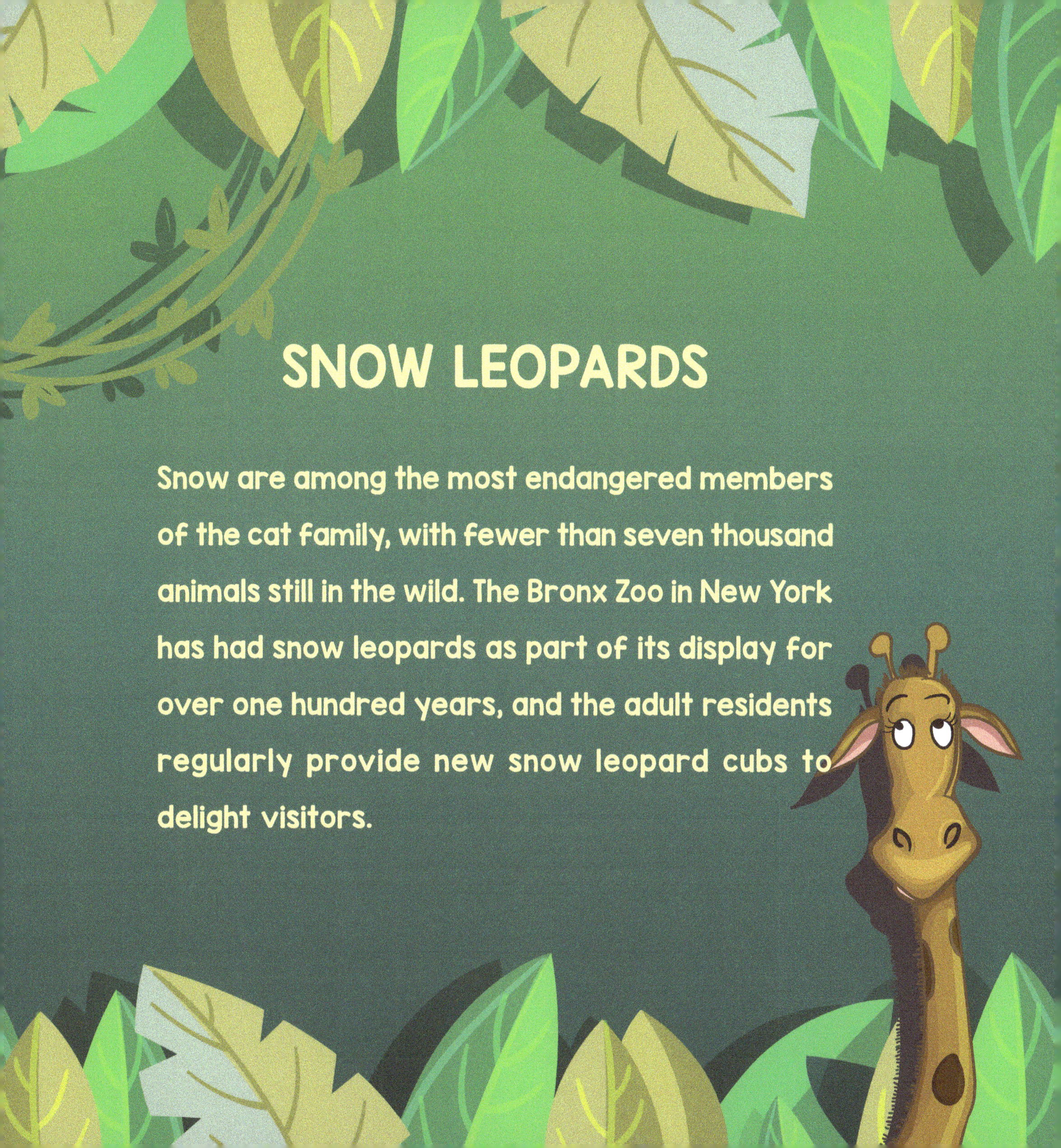

SNOW LEOPARDS

Snow are among the most endangered members of the cat family, with fewer than seven thousand animals still in the wild. The Bronx Zoo in New York has had snow leopards as part of its display for over one hundred years, and the adult residents regularly provide new snow leopard cubs to delight visitors.

PANAMANIAN GOLDEN FROG

There may be no more of these frogs outside of captivity now, due to climate change, pollution, and loss of habitat. Specimens like the frogs at the Maryland Zoo are therefore specially rare and precious.

Panamanian Golden Frog

Bactrian Camel

BACTRIAN CAMEL

Bactrian camels are the ones with a single hump. They normally live in the Gobi Desert in Asia, but wild Bactrian camels have almost disappeared. You can visit Bactrian camels at the Minnesota, Detroit, and San Diego zoos.

COTTON-TOP TAMARIN

Tamarins normally live in the rainforests of northern South America, but they have been heavily hunted to be sold as pets and are now almost extinct. The Lincoln Park Zoo in Illinois has several tamarins, and is working to keep the species from dying out.

Cotton-Top Tamarin

Lord Howe Island Stick Insect

LORD HOWE ISLAND STICK INSECT

This insect is also known as the tree lobster. It is native to an island in the Pacific Ocean, and scientists thought it had become extinct when rats came to the island on trading ships in the nineteenth century. There may be fewer than 30 of the insects left. The Melbourne Zoo in Australia and the San Diego Zoo in the United States both have examples of this rare insect.

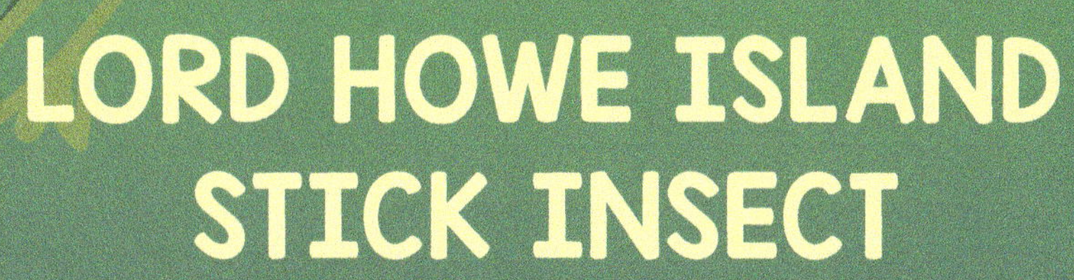

SUMATRAN TIGER

There are fewer than 300 Sumatran tigers left in Indonesia, so the few in zoos around the world are very important. The London Zoo was very pleased when one of its females had three babies in 2012.

BURMESE STAR TORTOISE

These tortoises are dying out as they are hunted for food. The Toronto Zoo in Canada has several tortoises and is hoping to breed more.

Some species are so rare that you may never find them in their natural homes. Sometimes only zoos keep species from becoming extinct.

New Guinea Singing Dog

NEW GUINEA SINGING DOG

There are several of these dogs in zoos around the world, but they all come from a very few parents. That means their genetic information is unstable, and they may not be able to continue their species. No singing dogs have been found in the wild since 1970.

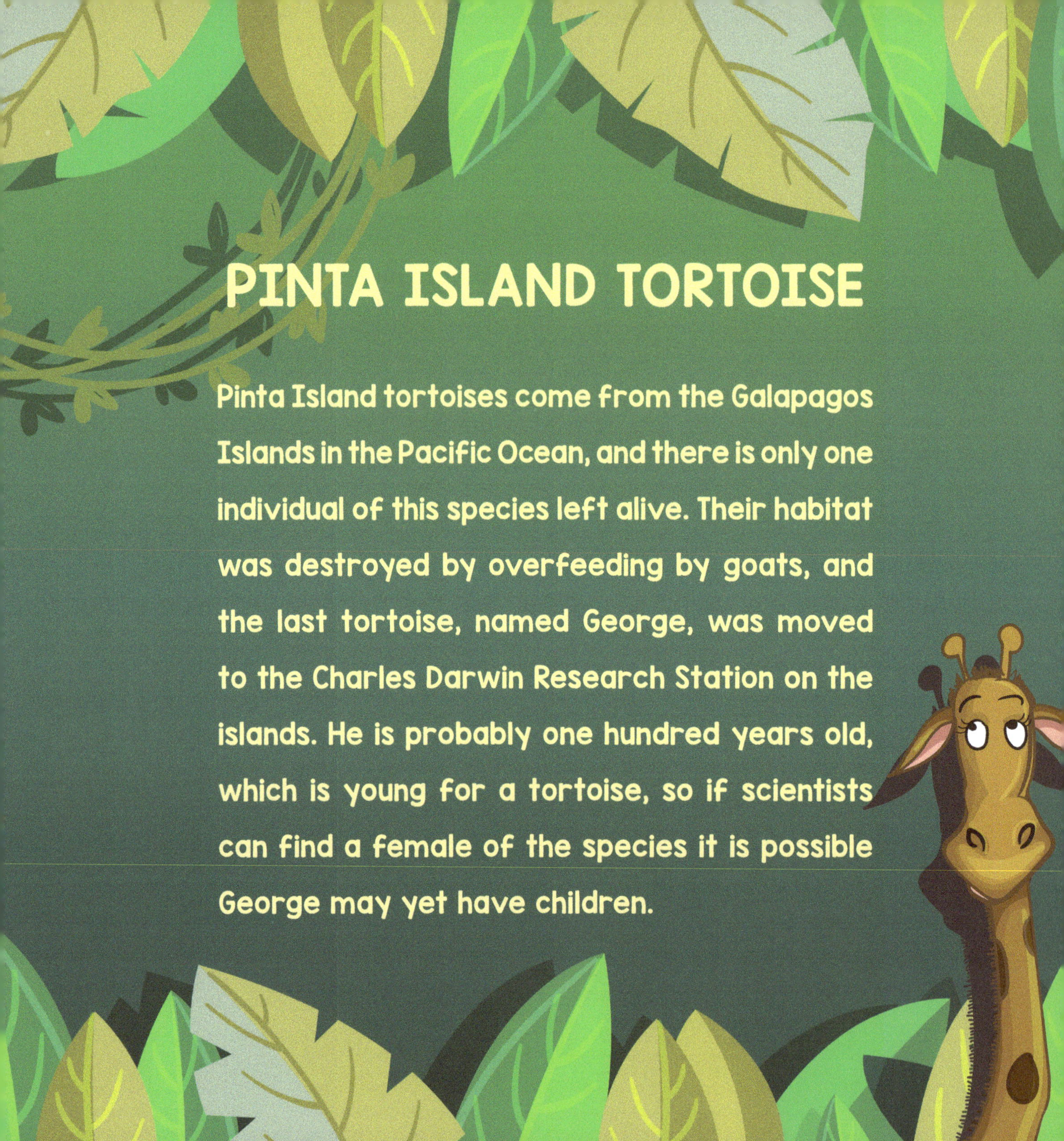

PINTA ISLAND TORTOISE

Pinta Island tortoises come from the Galapagos Islands in the Pacific Ocean, and there is only one individual of this species left alive. Their habitat was destroyed by overfeeding by goats, and the last tortoise, named George, was moved to the Charles Darwin Research Station on the islands. He is probably one hundred years old, which is young for a tortoise, so if scientists can find a female of the species it is possible George may yet have children.

Pinta Island Tortoise

Kihansi Spray Toad

KIHANSI SPRAY TOAD

This toad normally lives in the "spray zone", the wet area around two waterfalls in Tanzania in Africa. The water spray gives the toads their oxygen. When a dam was completed in the river above the waterfalls, and the spray from the waterfalls reduced, the toad population collapsed. We do not know of any left in the wild, so the toads in zoos around the world are the last representatives of their species. You can visit them at the Toledo, Chattanooga, and Bronx Zoos in the United States.

Zoos help us learn about creatures we could never
visit in the wild, and actually help other species avoid
becoming extinct. Read more about their work in the
Baby Professor book Should You Put Them in a Zoo?

Visit

BABY PROFESSOR
EDUCATION KIDS

www.BabyProfessorBooks.com

to download Free Baby Professor eBooks
and view our catalog of new and exciting
Children's Books